WHY GO TO COLLEGE?

This edition published by Lector House in 2024

ISBN: 978-93-6138-193-5
Edition copyright © 2024 by Lector House LLP

Lector House LLP
Registered Office: H. No. 96, Block C, Tomar Colony,
Burari, Delhi – 110084, India
info@lectorhouse.com
www.lectorhouse.com

WHY GO TO COLLEGE?

ALICE FREEMAN PALMER

2024

LECTOR HOUSE
LECTOR HOUSE LLP

WHY GO TO COLLEGE?
AN ADDRESS

BY

ALICE FREEMAN PALMER

FORMERLY PRESIDENT OF WELLESLEY COLLEGE

Why Go to College?

To a largely increasing number of young girls college doors are opening every year. Every year adds to the number of men who feel as a friend of mine, a successful lawyer in a great city, felt when in talking of the future of his four little children he said, "For the two boys it is not so serious, but I lie down at night afraid to die and leave my daughters only a bank account." Year by year, too, the experiences of life are teaching mothers that happiness does not necessarily come to their daughters when accounts are large and banks are sound, but that on the contrary they take grave risks when they trust everything to accumulated wealth and the chance of a happy marriage. Our American girls themselves are becoming aware that they need the stimulus, the discipline, the knowledge, the interests of the college in addition to the school, if they are to prepare themselves for the most serviceable lives.

But there are still parents who say, "There is no need that my daughter should teach; then why should she go to college?" I will not reply that college training is a life insurance for a girl, a pledge that she possesses the disciplined ability to earn a living for herself and others in case of need, for I prefer to insist on the importance of giving every girl, no matter what her present circumstances, a special training in some one thing by which she can render society service, not amateur but of an expert sort, and service too for which it will be willing to pay a price. The number of families will surely increase who will follow the example of an eminent banker whose daughters have been given each her specialty. One has chosen music, and has gone far with the best masters in this country and in Europe, so far that she now holds a high rank among musicians at home and abroad. Another has taken art, and has not been content to paint pretty gifts for her friends, but in the studios of New York, Munich, and Paris, she has won the right to be called an artist, and in her studio at home to paint portraits which have a market value. A third has proved that she can earn her living, if need be, by her exquisite jellies, preserves, and sweetmeats. Yet the house in the mountains, the house by the sea, and the friends in the city are not neglected, nor are these young women found less attractive because of their special accomplishments.

While it is not true that all girls should go to college any more than that all boys should go, it is nevertheless true that they should go in greater numbers than at present. They fail to go because they, their parents and their teachers, do not see clearly the personal benefits distinct from the commercial value of a college training. I wish here to discuss these benefits, these larger gifts of the college life,—what they may be, and for whom they are waiting.

It is undoubtedly true that many girls are totally unfitted by home and school life for a valuable college course. These joys and successes, these high interests and friendships, are not for the self-conscious and nervous invalid, nor for her who in the exuberance of youth recklessly ignores the laws of a healthy life. The good society of scholars and of libraries and laboratories has no place and no attraction for her who finds no message in Plato, no beauty in mathematical order, and who never longs to know the meaning of the stars over her head or the flowers under her feet. Neither will the finer opportunities of college life appeal to one who, until she is eighteen (is there such a girl in this country?), has felt no passion for the service of others, no desire to know if through history or philosophy, or any study of the laws of society, she can learn why the world is so sad, so hard, so selfish as she finds it, even when she looks upon it from the most sheltered life. No, the college cannot be, should not try to be, a substitute for the hospital, reformatory or kindergarten. To do its best work it should be organized for the strong, not for the weak; for the high-minded, self-controlled, generous, and courageous spirits, not for the indifferent, the dull, the idle, or those who are already forming their characters on the amusement theory of life. All these perverted young people may, and often do, get large benefit and invigoration, new ideals, and unselfish purposes from their four years' companionship with teachers and comrades of a higher physical, mental, and moral stature than their own. I have seen girls change so much in college that I have wondered if their friends at home would know them,—the voice, the carriage, the unconscious manner, all telling a story of new tastes and habits and loves and interests, that had wrought out in very truth a new creature. Yet in spite of this I have sometimes thought that in college more than elsewhere the old law holds, "To him that hath shall be given and he shall have abundance, but from him who hath not shall be taken away even that which he seemeth to have." For it is the young life which is open and prepared to receive which obtains the gracious and uplifting influences of college days. What, then, for such persons are the rich and abiding rewards of study in college or university?

Pre-eminently the college is a place of education. That is the ground of its being. We go to college to know, assured that knowledge is sweet and powerful, that a good education emancipates the mind and makes us citizens of the world. No college which does not thoroughly educate can be called good, no matter what else it does. No student who fails to get a little knowledge on many subjects, and much knowledge on some, can be said to have succeeded, whatever other advantages she may have found by the way. It is a beautiful and significant fact that in all times the years of learning have been also the years of romance. Those who love girls and boys pray that our colleges may be homes of sound learning, for knowledge is the condition of every college blessing. "Let no man incapable of mathematics enter here," Plato is reported to have inscribed over his Academy door. "Let no one to whom hard study is repulsive hope for anything from us," American colleges might paraphrase. Accordingly in my talk today I shall say little of the direct benefits of knowledge which the college affords. These may be assumed. It is on their account that one knocks at the college door. But seeking this first, a good many other things are added. I want to point out some of these collateral advantages of going to college, or rather to draw attention to some of the many forms in which the winning of knowledge presents itself.

The first of these is happiness. Everybody wants "a good time," especially every girl in her teens. A good time, it is true, does not always in these years mean what it will mean by and by, any more than the girl of eighteen plays with the doll which entranced the child of eight. It takes some time to discover that work is the best sort of play, and some people never discover it at all. But when mothers ask such questions as these: "How can I make my daughter happy?" "How can I give her the best society?" "How can she have a good time?" the answer in most cases is simple. Send her to college,—to almost any college. Send her because there is no other place where between eighteen and twenty-two she is so likely to have a genuinely good time. Merely for good times, for romance, for society, college life offers unequalled opportunities. Of course no idle person can possibly be happy, even for a day, nor she who makes a business of trying to amuse herself. For full happiness, though its springs are within, we want health and friends and work and objects of aspiration. "We live by admiration, hope, and love," says Wordsworth. The college abounds in all three. In the college time new powers are sprouting, and intelligence, merriment, truthfulness and generosity are more natural than the opposite qualities often become in later years. An exhilarating atmosphere pervades the place. We who are in it all the time feel that we live at the fountain of perpetual youth, and those who take but a four years' bath in it become more cheerful, strong, and full of promise than they are ever likely to find themselves again; for a college is a kind of compendium of the things that most men long for. It is usually planted in a beautiful spot, the charm of trees and water being added to stately buildings and stimulating works of art. Venerable associations of the past hallow its halls. Leaders in the stirring world of to-day return at each commencement to share the fresh life of the new class. Books, pictures, music, collections, appliances in every field, learned teachers, mirthful friends, athletics for holidays, the best words of the best men for holy days,—all are here. No wonder that men look back upon their college life as upon halcyon days, the romantic period of youth. No wonder that Dr. Holmes's poems to his Harvard classmates find an echo in college reunions everywhere; and gray-haired men, who outside the narrowing circle of home have not heard their first names for years, remain Bill and Joe and John and George to college comrades, even if unseen for more than a generation.

Yet a girl should go to college not merely to obtain four happy years but to make a second gain, which is often overlooked, and is little understood even when perceived; I mean a gain in health. The old notion that low vitality is a matter of course with women; that to be delicate is a mark of superior refinement, especially in well-to-do families; that sickness is a dispensation of Providence,—these notions meet with no acceptance in college. Years ago I saw in the mirror frame of a college freshman's room this little formula: "Sickness is carelessness, carelessness is selfishness, and selfishness is sin." And I have often noticed among college girls an air of humiliation and shame when obliged to confess a lack of physical vigor, as if they were convicted of managing life with bad judgment, or of some moral delinquency. With the spreading scientific conviction that health is a matter largely under each person's control, that even inherited tendencies to disease need not be allowed to run their riotous course unchecked, there comes an earnest purpose to be strong and free. Fascinating fields of knowledge are waiting to be explored; possibilities of doing, as well as of knowing, are on every side; new and dear friendships enlarge and sweeten dreams of future study and work, and the young student cannot afford quivering nerves or small lungs or an aching head any more than bad taste, rough manners, or a weak will. Handicapped by inheritance or bad training, she finds the plan of college life itself her supporter and friend. The steady, long-continued routine of mental work, physical exercise, recreation, and sleep, the simple and wholesome food, in place of irregular and unstudied diet, work out salvation for her. Instead of being left to go out-of-doors when she feels like it, the regular training of the gymnasium, the boats on lake and river, the tennis court, the golf links, the basket ball, the bicycle, the long walk among the woods in search of botanical or geological specimens,—all these and many more call to the busy student, until she realizes that they have their rightful place in every well-ordered day of every month. So she learns, little by little, that buoyant health is a precious possession to be won and kept.

It is significant that already statistical investigation in this country and in England shows that the standard of health is higher among the women who hold college degrees than among any other equal number of the same age and class. And it is interesting also to observe to what sort of questions our recent girl graduates have been inclined to devote attention. They have been largely the neglected problems of little children and their health, of home sanitation, of food and its choice and preparation, of domestic service, of the cleanliness of schools and public buildings. Colleges for girls are pledged by their very constitution to make persistent war on the water cure, the nervine retreat, the insane asylum, the hospital,—those bitter fruits of the emotional lives of thousands of women. "I can never afford a sick headache again, life is so interesting and there is so much to do," a delicate girl said to me at the end of her first college year. And while her mother was in a far-off invalid retreat, she undertook the battle against fate with the same intelligence and courage which she put into her calculus problems and her translations of Sophocles. Her beautiful home and her rosy and happy children prove the measure of her hard-won success. Formerly the majority of physicians had but one question for the mother of the nervous and delicate girl, "Does she go to school?" And only one prescription, "Take her out of school." Never a suggestion as to suppers of pickles and pound-cake, never a hint about midnight dancing and hurried day-time ways. But now the sensible doctor asks, "What are her interests? What are her tastes? What are her habits?" And he finds new interests for her, and urges the formation of out-of-door tastes and steady occupation for the mind, in order to draw the morbid girl from herself into the invigorating world outside. This the college does largely through its third gift of friendship.

Until a girl goes away from home to school or college, her friends are chiefly chosen for her by circumstances. Her young relatives, her neighbors in the same street, those who happen to go to the same school or church,— these she makes her girlish intimates. She goes to college with the entire conviction, half unknown to herself, that her father's political party contains all the honest men, her mother's social circle all the true ladies, her church all the real saints of the community. And the smaller the town, the more absolute is her belief. But in college she finds that the girl who earned her scholarship in the village school sits beside the banker's daughter; the New England farmer's child rooms next the heiress of a Hawaiian sugar plantation; the daughters of the opposing candidates in a sharply fought election have grown great friends in college boats and laboratories; and before her diploma is won she realizes how much richer a world she lives in than she ever dreamed of at home. The wealth that lies in differences has dawned upon her vision. It is only when the rich and poor sit down together that either can understand how the Lord is the Maker of them all.

To-day above all things we need the influence of men and women of friendliness, of generous nature, of hospitality to new ideas, in short, of social imagination. But instead, we find each political party bitterly calling the other dishonest, each class suspicious of the intentions of the other, and in social life the pettiest standards of conduct. Is it not well for us that the colleges all over the country still offer to their fortunate students a society of the most democratic sort,—one in which a father's money, a mother's social position, can assure no distinction and make no close friends? Here capacity of every kind counts for its full value. Here enthusiasm waits to make heroes of those who can lead. Here charming manners, noble character, amiable temper, scholarly power, find their full opportunity and inspire such friendships as are seldom made afterward. I have forgotten my chemistry, and my classical philology cannot bear examination; but all round the world there are men and women at work, my intimates of college days, who have made the wide earth a friendly place to me. Of every creed, of every party, in far-away places and in near, the thought of them makes me more courageous in duty and more faithful to opportunity, though for many years we may not have had time to write each other a letter. The basis of all valuable and enduring friendships is not accident or juxtaposition, but tastes, interests, habits, work, ambitions. It is for this reason that to college friendship clings a romance entirely its own. One of the friends may spend her days in the laboratory, eagerly chasing the shy facts that hide beyond the microscope's fine vision, and the other may fill her hours and her heart with the poets and the philosophers; one may steadfastly pursue her way toward the command of a hospital, and the other towards the world of letters and of art; these divergences constitute no barrier, but rather an aid to the fulness of friendship. And the fact that one goes in a simple gown which she has earned and made herself, and the other lives when at home in a merchant's modern palace—what has that to do with the things the girls care about and the dreams they talk over in the walk by the river or the bicycle ride through country roads? If any young man to-day goes through Harvard lonely, neglected, unfriended, if any girl lives solitary and wretched in her life at Wellesley, it is their own fault. It must be because they are suspicious, unfriendly or disagreeable themselves. Certainly it is true that in the associations of college life, more than in any other that the country can show, what is extraneous, artificial, and temporary falls away, and the every-day relations of life and work take on a character that is simple, natural, genuine. And so it comes about that the fourth gift of college life is ideals of personal character.

To some people the shaping ideals of what character should be, often held unconsciously, come from the books they are given by the persons whom they most admire before they are twenty years old. The greatest thing any friend or teacher, either in school or college, can do for a student is to furnish him with a personal ideal. The college professors who transformed me through my acquaintance with them—ah, they were few, and I am sure I did not have a dozen conversations with them outside their class rooms— gave me, each in his different way, an ideal of character, of conduct, of the scholar, the leader, of which they and I were totally unconscious at the time. For many years I have known that my study with them, no matter whether of philosophy or of Greek, of mathematics or history or English, enlarged my notions of life, uplifted my standards of culture, and so inspired me with new possibilities of usefulness and of happiness. Not the facts and theories that I learned so much as the men who taught me, gave this inspiration. The community at large is right in saying that it wants the personal influence of professors on students, but it is wholly wrong in assuming that this precious influence comes from frequent meetings or talks on miscellaneous subjects. There is quite as likely to be a quickening force in the somewhat remote and mysterious power of the teacher who devotes himself to amassing treasures of scholarship, or to patiently working out the best methods of teaching; who standing somewhat apart, still remains an ideal of the Christian scholar, the just, the courteous man or woman. To come under the influence of one such teacher is enough to make college life worthwhile. A young man who came to Harvard with eighty cents in his pocket, and worked his way through, never a high scholar, and now in a business which looks very commonplace, told me the other day that he would not care to be alive if he had not gone to college. His face flushed as he explained how different his days would have been if he had not known two of his professors. "Do you use your college studies in your business?" I asked. "Oh, no!" he answered. "But I am another man in doing the business; and when the day's work is done I live another life because of my college experiences. The business and I are both the better for it every day." How many a young girl has had her whole horizon extended by the changed ideals she gained in college! Yet this is largely because the associations and studies there are likely to give her permanent interests—the fifth and perhaps the greatest gift of college life of which I shall speak.

The old fairy story which charmed us in childhood ended with—"And they were married and lived happy ever after." It conducted to the altar, having brought the happy pair through innumerable difficulties, and left us with the contented sense that all the mistakes and problems would now vanish and life be one long day of unclouded bliss. I have seen devoted and intelligent mothers arrange their young daughters' education and companionships precisely on this basis. They planned as if these pretty and charming girls were going to live only twenty or twenty-five years at the utmost, and had consequently no need of the wealthy interests that should round out the full-grown woman's stature, making her younger in feeling at forty than at twenty, and more lovely and admired at eighty than at either.

Emerson in writing of beauty declares that "the secret of ugliness consists not in irregular outline, but in being uninteresting. We love any forms, however ugly, from which great qualities shine. If command, eloquence, art, or invention exists in the most deformed person, all the accidents that usually displease, please, and raise esteem and wonder higher. Beauty without grace is the head without the body. Beauty without expression tires." Of course such considerations can hardly come with full force to the young girl herself, who feels aged at eighteen, and imagines that the troubles and problems of life and thought are hers already. "Oh, tell me to-night," cried a college freshman once to her President, "which is the right side and which is the wrong side of this Andover question about eschatology?" The young girl is impatient of open questions, and irritated at her inability to answer them. Neither can she believe that the first headlong zest with which she throws herself into society, athletics, into everything which comes in her way, can ever fail. But her elders know, looking on, that our American girl, the comrade of her parents and of her brothers and their friends, brought up from babyhood in the eager talk of politics and society, of religious belief, of public action, of social responsibility—that this typical girl, with her quick sympathies, her clear head, her warm heart, her outreaching hands, will not permanently be satisfied or self-respecting, though she have the prettiest dresses and hats in town, or the most charming of dinners, dances, and teas. Unless there comes to her, and comes early, the one chief happiness of life,—a marriage of comradeship,—she must face for herself the question, "What shall I do with my life?"

I recall a superb girl of twenty as I overtook her one winter morning hurrying along Commonwealth Avenue. She spoke of a brilliant party at a friend's the previous evening. "But, oh!" she cried, throwing up her hands in a kind of hopeless impatience, "tell me what to do. My dancing days are over!" I laughed at her, "Have you sprained your ankle?" But I saw I had made a mistake when she added, "It is no laughing matter. I have been out three years. I have not done what they expected of me," with a flush and a shrug, "and there is a crowd of nice girls coming on this winter; and anyway, I am so tired of going to teas and ball-games and assemblies! I don't care the least in the world for foreign missions, and," with a stamp, "I am not going slumming among the Italians. I have too much respect for the Italians. And what shall I do with the rest of my life?" That was a frank statement of what any girl of brains or conscience feels, with more or less bitter distinctness, unless she marries early, or has some pressing work for which she is well trained.

Yet even if that which is the profession of woman *par excellence* be hers, how can she be perennially so interesting a companion to her husband and children as if she had keen personal tastes, long her own, and growing with her growth? Indeed, in that respect the condition of men is almost the same as that of women. It would be quite the same were it not for the fact that a man's business or profession is generally in itself a means of growth, of education, of dignity. He leans his life against it. He builds his home in the shadow of it. It binds his days together in a kind of natural piety and makes him advance in strength and nobility as he "fulfils the common round, the daily task." And that is the reason why men in the past, if they have been honorable men, have grown old better than women. Men usually retain their ability longer, their mental alertness and hospitality. They add fine quality to fine quality, passing from strength to strength and preserving in old age whatever has been best in youth. It was a sudden recognition of this fact which made a young friend of mine say last winter, "I am not going to parties any more; the men best worth talking with are too old to dance."

Even with the help of a permanent business or profession, however, the most interesting men I know are those who have an avocation as well as a vocation. I mean a taste or work quite apart from the business of life. This revives, inspires, and cultivates them perpetually. It matters little what it is, if only it is real and personal, is large enough to last, and possesses the power of growth. A young sea-captain from a New England village on a long and lonely voyage falls upon a copy of Shelley. Appeal is made to his fine but untrained mind, and the book of the boy poet becomes the seaman's university. The wide world of poetry and of the other fine arts is opened, and the Shelleyian specialist becomes a cultivated, original, and charming man. A busy merchant loves flowers, and in all his free hours studies them. Each new spring adds knowledge to his knowledge, and his friends continually bring him their strange discoveries. With growing wealth he cultivates rare and beautiful plants, and shares them with his fortunate acquaintances. Happy the companion invited to a walk or a drive with such observant eyes, such vivid talk! Because of this cheerful interest in flowers, and this ingenious skill in dealing with them, the man himself is interesting. All his powers are alert, and his judgment is valued in public life and in private business. Or is it more exact to say that because he is the kind of man who would insist upon having such interests outside his daily work, he is still fresh and young and capable of growth at an age when many other men are dull and old and certain that the time of decay is at hand?

There are two reasons why women need to cultivate these large and abiding interests even more persistently than men. In the first place, they have more leisure. They are indeed the only leisure class in the country, the only large body of persons who are not called upon to win their daily bread in direct wage-earning ways. As yet, fortunately, few men among us have so little self-respect as to idle about our streets and drawing-rooms because their fathers are rich enough to support them. We are not without our unemployed poor; but roving tramps and idle clubmen are after all not of large consequence. Our serious, non-producing classes are chiefly women. It is the regular ambition of the chivalrous American to make all the women who depend on him so comfortable that they need do nothing for themselves. Machinery has taken nearly all the former occupations of women out of the home into the shop and factory. Widespread wealth and comfort, and the inherited theory that it is not well for the woman to earn money so long as father or brothers can support her, have brought about a condition of things in which there is social danger, unless with the larger leisure are given high and enduring interests. To health especially there is great danger, for nothing breaks down a woman's health like idleness and its resulting *ennui*. More people, I am sure, are broken down nervously because they are bored, than because they are overworked; and more still go to pieces through fussiness, unwholesome living, worry over petty details, and the daily disappointments which result from small and superficial training. And then, besides the danger to health, there is the danger to character. I need not dwell on the undermining influence which men also feel when occupation is taken away and no absorbing private interest fills the vacancy. The vices of luxurious city life are perhaps hardly more destructive to character than is the slow deterioration of barren country life. Though the conditions in the two cases are exactly opposite, the trouble is often the same,—absence of noble interests. In the city restless idleness organizes amusement; in the country deadly dulness succeeds daily toil.

But there is a second reason why a girl should acquire for herself strong and worthy interests. The regular occupations of women in their homes are generally disconnected and of little educational value, at least as those homes are at present conducted. Given the best will in the world, the daily doing of household details becomes a wearisome monotony if the mere performance of them is all. To make drudgery divine a woman must have a brain to plan and eyes to see how to "sweep a room as to God's laws." Imagination and knowledge should be the hourly companions of her who would make a fine art of each detail in kitchen and nursery. Too long has the pin been the appropriate symbol of the average woman's life—the pin, which only temporarily holds together things which may or may not have any organic connection with one another. While undoubtedly most women must spend the larger part of life in this modest pin-work, holding together the little things of home and school and society and church, it is also true, that cohesive work itself cannot be done well, even in humble circumstances, except by the refined, the trained, the growing woman. The smallest village, the plainest home, give ample space for the resources of the trained college woman. And the reason why such homes and such villages are so often barren of grace and variety is just because these fine qualities have not ruled them. The higher graces of civilization halt among us; dainty and finished ways of living give place to common ways, while vulgar tastes, slatternly habits, clouds and despondency reign in the house. Little children under five years of age die in needless thousands because of the dull, unimaginative women on whom they depend. Such women have been satisfied with just getting along, instead of packing everything they do with brains, instead of studying the best possible way of doing everything small or large; for there is always a best way, whether of setting a table, of trimming a hat, or teaching a child to read. And this taste for perfection can be cultivated; indeed, it must be cultivated, if our standards of living are to be raised. There is now scientific knowledge enough, there is money enough, to prevent the vast majority of the evils which afflict our social organism, if mere knowledge or wealth could avail; but the greater difficulty is to make intelligence, character, good taste, unselfishness prevail.

What, then, are the interests which powerfully appeal to mind and heart, and so are fitted to become the strengthening companions of a woman's life? I shall mention only three, all of them such as are elaborately fostered by college life. The first is the love of great literature. I do not mean that use of books by which a man may get what is called a good education and so be better qualified for the battle of life, nor do I mention books in their character as reservoirs of knowledge, books which we need for special purposes, and which are no longer of consequence when our purpose with them is served. I have in mind the great books, especially the great poets, books to be adopted as a resource and a solace. The chief reason why so many people do not know how to make comrades of such books is because they have come to them too late. We have in this country enormous numbers of readers, probably a larger number who read, and who read many hours in the week, than has ever been known elsewhere in the world. But what do these millions read besides the newspapers? Possibly a denominational religious weekly and another journal of fashion or business. Then come the thousands who read the best magazines, and whatever else is for the moment popular in novels and poetry—the last dialect story, the fashionable poem, the questionable but talked-of novel. Let a violent attack be made on the decency of a new story and instantly, if only it is clever, its author becomes famous.

But the fashions in reading of a restless race—the women too idle, the men too heavily worked—I will not discuss here. Let light literature be devourered by our populace as his drug is taken by the opium-eater, and with a similar narcotic effect. We can only seek out the children, and hope by giving them from babyhood bits of the noblest literature, to prepare them for the great opportunities of mature life. I urge, therefore, reading as a mental stimulus, as a solace in trouble, a perpetual source of delight; and I would point out that we must not delay to make the great friendships that await us on the library shelves until sickness shuts the door on the outer world, or death enters the home and silences the voices that once helped to make these friendships sweet. If Homer and Shakespeare and Wordsworth and Browning are to have meaning for us when we need them most, it will be because they come to us as old familiar friends whose influences have permeated the glad and busy days before. The last time I heard James Russell Lowell talk to college girls, he said,—for he was too ill to say many words—"I have only this one message to leave with you. In all your work in college never lose sight of the reason why you have come here. It is not that you may get something by which to earn your bread, but that every mouthful of bread may be the sweeter to your taste."

And this is the power possessed by the mighty dead,—men of every time and nation, whose voices death cannot silence, who are waiting even at the poor man's elbow, whose illuminating words may be had for the price of a day's work in the kitchen or the street, for lack of love of whom many a luxurious home is a dull and solitary spot, breeding misery and vice. Now the modern college is especially equipped to introduce its students to such literature. The library is at last understood to be the heart of the college. The modern librarian is not the keeper of books, as was his predecessor, but the distributer of them, and the guide to their resources, proud when he increases the use of his treasures. Every language, ancient or modern, which contains a literature is now taught in college. Its history is examined, its philology, its masterpieces, and more than ever is English literature studied and loved. There is now every opportunity for the college student to become an expert in the use of his own tongue and pen. What other men painfully strive for he can enjoy to the full with comparatively little effort.

But there is a second invigorating interest to which college training introduces its student. I mean the study of nature, intimacy with the strange and beautiful world in which we live. "Nature never did betray the heart that loved her," sang her poet high priest. When the world has been too much with us, nothing else is so refreshing to tired eyes and mind as woods and water, and an intelligent knowledge of the life within them. For a generation past there has been a well-nigh universal turning of the population toward the cities. In 1840 only nine per cent of our people lived in cities of 8,000 inhabitants or more. Now more than a third of us are found in cities. But the electric-car, the telephone, the bicycle, still keep avenues to the country open. Certain it is that city people feel a growing hunger for the country, particularly when grass begins to grow. This is a healthy taste, and must increase the general knowledge and love of nature. Fortunate are the little children in those schools whose teachers know and love the world in which they live. Their young eyes are early opened to the beauty of birds and trees and plants. Not only should we expect our girls to have a feeling for the fine sunset or the wide-reaching panorama of field and water, but to know something also about the less obvious aspects of nature, its structure, its methods of work, and the endless diversity of its parts. No one can have read Matthew Arnold's letters to his wife, his mother, and his sister, without being struck by the immense enjoyment he took throughout his singularly simple and hard-working life in flowers and trees and rivers. The English lake country had given him this happy inheritance, with everywhere its sound of running water and its wealth of greenery. There is a close connection between the marvellous unbroken line of English song, and the passionate love of the Englishman for a home in the midst of birds, trees, and green fields.

> "The world is so full of a number of things,
> That I think we should all be as happy as kings,"

is the opinion of everybody who knows nature as did Robert Louis Stevenson. And so our college student may begin to know it. Let her enter the laboratories and investigate for herself. Let her make her delicate experiments with the blowpipe or the balance; let her track mysterious life from one hiding-place to another; let her "name all the birds without a gun," and make intimates of flower and fish and butterfly—and she is dull indeed if breezy tastes do not follow her through life, and forbid any of her days to be empty of intelligent enjoyment. "Keep your years beautiful; make your own atmosphere," was the parting advice of my college president, himself a living illustration of what he said.

But it is a short step from the love of the complex and engaging world in which we live to the love of our comrades in it. Accordingly the third precious interest to be cultivated by the college student is an interest in people. The scholar today is not a being who dwells apart in his cloister, the monk's successor; he is a leader of the thoughts and conduct of men.

So the new subjects which stand beside the classics and mathematics of medieval culture are history, economics, ethics, and sociology. Although these subjects are as yet merely in the making, thousands of students are flocking to their investigation, and are going out to try their tentative knowledge in College Settlements and City Missions and Children's Aid Societies. The best instincts of generous youth are becoming enlisted in these living themes. And why should our daughters remain aloof from the most absorbing work of modern city life, work quite as fascinating to young women as to young men? During many years of listening to college sermons and public lectures in Wellesley, I always noticed a quickened attention in the audience whenever the discussion touched politics or theology. These are, after all, the permanent and peremptory interests, and they should be given their full place in a healthy and vigorous life.

But if that life includes a love of books, of nature, of people, it will naturally turn to enlarged conceptions of religion—my sixth and last gift of college life. In his first sermon as Master of Balliol College, Dr. Jowett spoke of the college, "First as a place of education, secondly as a place of society, thirdly as a place of religion." He observed that "men of very great ability often fail in life because they are unable to play their part with effect. They are shy, awkward, self-conscious, deficient in manners, faults which are as ruinous as vices." The supreme end of college training, he said, "is usefulness in after life." Similarly, when the city of Cambridge celebrated in Harvard's Memorial Hall the life and death of the gallant young ex-governor of Massachusetts, William E. Russell, men did well to hang above his portrait some wise words he has lately said, "Never forget the everlasting difference between making a living and making a life." That he himself never forgot; and it was well to remind citizens and students of it, as they stood there facing too the ancient words all Harvard men face when they take their college degrees and go out into the world, "They that be wise shall shine as the brightness of the firmament, and they that turn many to righteousness as the stars for ever and ever." Good words these to go out from college with. The girls of Wellesley gather every morning at chapel to bow their heads together for a moment before they scatter among the libraries and lecture-rooms and begin the experiments of the new day. And always their college motto meets the eyes that are raised to its penetrating message, "Not to be ministered unto, but to minister." How many a young heart has loyally responded, "And to give life a ransom for many." That is the "Wellesley spirit;" and the same sweet spirit of devout service has gone forth from all our college halls. In any of them one may catch the echo of Whittier's noble psalm,—

"O Lord and Master of us all
Whate'er our name or sign,
We own Thy sway, we hear Thy call,
We test our lives by Thine."

That is the supreme test of life,—its consecrated serviceableness. The Master of Balliol was right; the brave men and women who founded our schools and colleges were not wrong. "For Christ and the Church" universities were set up in the wilderness of New England; for the large service of the State they have been founded and maintained at public cost in every section of the country where men have settled, from the Alleghanies across the prairies· and Rocky Mountains down to the Golden Gate. Founded primarily as seats of learning, their teachers have been not only scientists and linguists, philosophers and historians, but men and women of holy purposes, sound patriotism, courageous convictions, refined and noble tastes. Set as these teachers have been upon a hill, their light has at no period of our country's history been hid. They have formed a large factor in our civilization, and in their own beautiful characters have continually shown us how to combine religion and life, the ideal and practical, the human and the divine.

Such are some of the larger influences to be had from college life. It is true all the good gifts I have named may be secured without the aid of the college. We all know young men and women who have had no college training, who are as cultivated, rational, resourceful, and happy as any people we know, who excel in every one of these particulars the college graduates about them. I believe they often bitterly regret the lack of a college education. And we see young men and women going through college deaf and blind to their great chances there, and afterwards curiously careless and wasteful of the best things in life. While all this is true, it is true too that to the open-minded and ambitious boy or girl of moderate health, ability, self-control, and studiousness, a college course offers the most attractive, easy, and probable way of securing happiness and health, good friends and high ideals, permanent interests of a noble kind, and large capacity for usefulness in the world. It has been well said that the ability to see great things large and little things small is the final test of education. The foes of life, especially of women's lives, are caprice, wearisome incapacity and petty judgments. From these oppressive foes we long to escape to the rule of right reason, where all things are possible, and life becomes a glory instead of a grind. No college, with the best teachers and collections in the world, can by its own power impart all this to any woman. But if one has set her face in that direction, where else can she find so many hands reached out to help, so many encouraging voices in the air, so many favoring influences filling the days and nights?